Original title:
The Houseplant Diaries

Copyright © 2025 Creative Arts Management OÜ
All rights reserved.

Author: Gabriel Kingsley
ISBN HARDBACK: 978-1-80581-716-1
ISBN PAPERBACK: 978-1-80581-243-2
ISBN EBOOK: 978-1-80581-716-1

Vines of Yesterday

In a corner, green vines twist,
A high and lofty trellis missed.
I swear I fed it, don't you think?
But it's on the fridge; it likes to drink.

Every leaf a story, it gleams,
Of lost hopes and awkward dreams.
Dancing in the sunlight, it may,
But also plotting my dismay.

Breaths Between Blooms

A cactus sits, sharp and sly,
Pretending it's a lullaby.
With every poke, it sings with glee,
'You can't hug me! Just wait and see!'

In the silence, whispers grow,
While petunias start their grand show.
I chuckle at the blooms so bold,
Yet last week, they were looking cold.

Blooms in the Basement

In the depths where shadows creep,
I parked some flowers for a sleep.
They giggle softly, it's quite the sight,
As I forget, they need some light.

With dust bunnies as their friends,
They plan the party that never ends.
Pansies waltz, while ferns partake,
A basement rave; make no mistake!

Nature's Color Palette

My plant is getting quite the glow,
From a pot that's waaaay too low.
Golden leaves and stems so bright,
   I may just hang it up tonight!

It claims it hates too much sun,
But when it blooms, oh what fun!
Each color shines, flamboyant, loud,
   I walk past, feeling quite proud.

Tending to the Green

Water, mist, and sunlight, too,
My leafy friends are quite the crew.
They whisper secrets, beg for snacks,
Oh dear, they think I'm their own chef!

Fertilizer is a scent divine,
But my nose says, 'Keep that out, it's mine!'
Yet as they drink their rich buffet,
I wonder if plants have a buffet day.

The Light of Lushness

In the corner, a fern starts to sway,
It dances like it knows ballet.
The cactus sits with prickly pride,
While I just hope it won't decide!

Sunbeams bounce around with glee,
As leaves perform a canopy.
I've opened windows, given them space,
Each plant saying, 'Thanks, now we embrace!'

Tapestries of Tendrils

My ivy climbs the walls so bold,
It seems to seek a life untold.
'Tell me your stories!' I shout and plead,
Yet all it says is, 'Just water, please!'

The philodendron, with colorful flair,
Grows wildly like it just doesn't care.
I trim and snip, but off it goes,
A runaway plant with extravagant prose!

A Sanctuary for Saplings

Little sprouts in a pot so tight,
They stretch for the moon, oh what a sight!
While I sit sipping my cup of tea,
They're plotting a take-over—oh, woe is me!

With each new leaf, they sing and cheer,
Like they've won a green trophy, oh dear!
In a wild kingdom, they rule with sass,
Awaiting the day they'll conquer my glass!

Conversations with Cacti

In the corner, spiky and green,
A cactus whispers, what does it mean?
"Don't poke the bear, or lose your mind,"
In this prickly chat, much fun I find.

Laughter echoes off the pot,
As I debate if he likes the spot.
"Just one more inch, please take a guess,"
"Or maybe I need a bit less stress?"

"My needles shine, I'm all the rage,"
"Oh cactus friend, you turn the page!"
"In a world of foliage, you're a king!"
As we swap tales of dingy and bling.

He claims he's tough, but I just smile,
With every jab, he's lost his style.
Two friends grown from soil and dream,
Together we flourish, or so it seems!

The Stillness of Succulents

In a sunny nook, they sit so still,
Potatoes of the plant world, oh what a thrill!
"How do you breathe with no rush or fuss?"
"I just soak up rays, don't make a fuss!"

With a gentle grin, they share their lore,
"We're champions of chill, we crave no more!"
Water once a month? Oh, what a breeze!
"A sprinkle of love, and we do as we please!"

Across the shelf, they flaunt their hues,
Greens to reds, in the sun-kissed views.
"We're not just pretty, there's talent here!"
"We drink your bad vibes, and turn them clear!"

In silent laughter, they sway like a dance,
No hurry or worry, just serendipity's chance.
They urge me to chill, to laugh, and to stay,
In their tranquil world, I lose my way!

Rhythm of Photosynthesis

Sunshine streaming, I've hit the groove,
Photosynthesis got me in the move!
"Let's throw a party, leave the darkness behind!"
"I'll take the sun, you bring the wind!"

With every ounce of light, we find the beat,
Dancing chlorophyll, can't resist that heat!
"Gas exchange? Oh, what a breeze!"
"Plant pals unite, let's sway with ease!"

They form the chorus, in green harmony,
Each leaf a note, in this symphony.
"Oxygen's the gift, we give and take!"
"Join the rhythm, for photosynthesis sake!"

In this leafy ballet, we twirl and spin,
Nature's great secret is where we begin.
Laughing at pollen and all it entails,
With every bright moment, our joy prevails!

Tales from the Terrarium

Inside this glass world, stories unfold,
With mossy carpets and treasures untold.
"Once upon a leaf, a mystery grew,"
"A tiny pea plant, with a point of view!"

"I once had a friend, a mischievous bug,
Who danced on my leaves, like a cozy snug!"
"Then came the rain, it was quite the show,"
"A flood of adventures, that charmed my glow!"

Under glass dome, we share our dreams,
With every raindrop, our laughter beams.
"Here lives my saga, come take a peek!"
"There's never a dull moment, just plant and cheek!"

So gather around, for tales to share,
Of leafy wonders, and love in the air.
In this humid realm, joy's the norm,
We're a quirky crew, forever warmed!

Eavesdropping on Eucalyptus

In the corner, Eucalyptus sneezes,
Pollen flies like it's a breeze.
"Bless you!" cries the fern next door,
"I thought you'd finally found a cure!"

Dancing leaves sway to the beat,
Rubber plant winks, oh what a treat.
"Tell us more!" they all demand,
"About that time you sunbathed unplanned!"

A story whispered in the light,
Of a spider who put up a fight.
"Boo!" he jumped, oh what a scene,
"Next time, I'll stick to the cuisine!"

Eucalyptus blushes, looks away,
Leaves rustle in the gossip's play.
Between each pot, they share their tales,
Of sunny days, and those rainy gales.

The Secret Life of Spathiphyllum

Spathiphyllum grins with grace,
Shyly hiding in its place.
"Do you know I speak in rain?"
"Whisper soft, and feel no pain!"

Eavesdropping on the sunlight's talk,
Bantering with shadows on the walk.
"I prefer the drip over the dry!"
"And those who forget to pass by!"

With its whites and greens so pristine,
Makes the other plants quite mean.
"Look at me, I'm picture perfect!"
Leaning in, feeling quite the misdirect!

Underneath that pretty veil,
Hides the truth, a secret trail.
With each sip from the watering can,
Lives a party no one can plan!

Notes from a Thriving Anthurium

Anthurium's got the flair,
Dazzling bright without a care.
"Is it me or the light?" it winks,
"These petals dance while the sunlight blinks!"

The neighbors stare, their envy clear,
"Could we borrow that charm, my dear?"
Crimson colors, leaf edges fine,
Muttering tales of "Look at mine!"

"I was born to be admired,"
The Anthurium boasts, never tired.
"I don't wilt; I just adore,"
"Every window, every door!"

So gather 'round, the leafy crew,
It's a plant's world, and it's true.
With every bloom, it shares a laugh,
In this green life, they're all a gaffe!

Ferns and Forgotten Corners

In forgotten corners, ferns do thrive,
Spreading green where bugs arrive.
"What's that? A spider? Oh no, please!"
"Not a dinner guest, let's take it with ease!"

With fronds unfurling, they seem to sway,
As if to say, "We like it this way!"
"Dust bunnies have taken our space!"
"Let's forge a plan; let's set our pace!"

Whispers of secrets in the air,
"Did you hear? They're trimming with flair!"
"Let them try, we'll still be here,"
"In this cozy spot, there's nothing to fear!"

So, ferns plotted in leafy glee,
Chasing dust and dreaming free.
In corners long lost to the light,
They weave their tales through the quiet night.

Memories in Moss

In corners where the sunlight creeps,
My mossy friend just quietly sleeps.
I swear it grins at every joke,
As I recall the plants I broke.

A fern once danced upon the shelf,
I laughed so hard, I lost myself.
The cactus quills, a prickly joke,
Regretted hugs were no fun, broke.

Each mossy patch, a glowy cheer,
That whispers tales I often hear.
Of leaves that fell and those that sprouted,
In my plant world, joy's never doubted.

Oh, the stories that we weave,
With tiny green friends up our sleeves.
In pots of humor, life's a blast,
Moments in moss — the best ones last.

The Pulse of Petals

The petals wave like they can sing,
In my living room, they do their thing.
A peace lily, flashing white,
Said, "Don't be shy, let's start the night!"

The daisies giggle, roots all entwined,
They plot with me — oh, how they're aligned!
I tell them secrets while I prune,
Their laughter fills the afternoon.

A tulip trips, a comical fall,
"Watch your step!" I hear them call.
In the dance of plants, you'll see it clear,
Life's a party, with petals near.

So let's keep blooming, day by day,
With pulse and petals leading the way.
In this funny tale, we're all aligned,
In the garden of giggles, joy we'll find.

Guardians in the Greenhouse

In the glasshouse, I'm the scribe,
With leafy guards, oh, what a vibe!
The snapdragon's judgment, sharp and quick,
While I try not to trip on sticks.

A rubber plant with an eyebrow raised,
Judges my choices, mildly amazed.
The geraniums gossip, green and bold,
Whispering tales of dirt and hold.

In the midst of flora, I feel so grand,
Yet they know all my secret plans.
I'm the human, yet they lead the show,
With guardians green, I'm never alone.

They keep my secrets, and though it's true,
They can't keep quiet, just like me too.
Together we laugh under the moon's glance,
In the greenhouse's laughter, we all dance.

A Symphony of Sprouts

In the window, sprouts begin to play,
A symphony of greens on display.
Each tiny leaf, a note in the air,
My living orchestra, beyond compare.

The basil leads with its fragrant tune,
While pea shoots sway, like dancers in June.
A note from spinach gives a deep sigh,
"Oh dear me, who let the weeds try?"

In rhythmic potting, we jam each day,
With laughter and soil, come what may.
Chorus of carrots, a rooty refrain,
In my home, their music can't be contained.

So here's to the sprouts, my lively crew,
Each with a part, making dreams come true.
In this symphony, we all take a bow,
Together in harmony, let's thrive, let's wow.

Breathing Life

My fern just gave me a wink,
I swear that plant can think.
It wants a snack, a sip, a hug,
I guess it's time to give it a tug.

The cactus rules with sharp-tongued flair,
It's got a prickly sense of care.
Don't ask for hugs, it won't comply,
A tiny joke, just let it lie.

The pothos climbs like it owns the place,
In every room, it finds a space.
With trailing vines, it makes a show,
Like a green-haired celebrity, in tow.

In this jungle, I'm their jester,
They laugh at me, their faithful tester.
Who knew that plants could have such fun?
And here I thought I was the one!

In the Shadows of Growth

Beneath the light, my plants conspire,
They whisper tales of soil and fire.
"Well, my leaves are shinier than yours!"
Said the succulent, while the sun out pours.

The spider plant threw a wild party,
And I, the host, felt far less hearty.
They danced and swayed, those leafy friends,
While I just sighed, and hoped it ends.

With laughs and jokes, they share the fun,
But every time I try, I run.
"Just add some water, it's not so tough!"
They say with glee, but I've had enough!

In shadows deep, they plot and scheme,
While I just try to live the dream.
These housemates green, what mischief they brew,
I'm just the one they pull into too!

Petals and Promises

In a pot, a blossom smiles bright,
"I promise to bloom once the sun's right!"
Yet here I stand, my patience thin,
Waiting for petals to finally begin.

The daisies giggle, they're all in bloom,
While I'm stuck here, filled with gloom.
"Just a bit longer!" they tease with grace,
I roll my eyes at their blooming race.

Begonias whisper secrets so sweet,
While I negotiate with my wilted seat.
"Just a sprinkle, just a love tap!"
But my watering can feels like a trap.

In the chaos of growth, I stand alone,
With a flower that still refuses to own.
Petals and promises float in the air,
"Just give it time!" they say with flair.

The Language of Leaves

In language of leaves, they chat all day,
A golden pothos takes the lead, hooray!
"What's the gossip from the window sill?"
"Oh, just the sun, it's giving a thrill!"

"Watch the spider plant, it's going wild,
A cascade of green, like a happy child!"
While I stand here, scratching my head,
Wondering what they've really said.

The ferns are shaking, they're telling a joke,
But I'm just trying to find where I broke.
"Your leaves are droopy, what's the deal?"
"Just sipping too much, what's the appeal?"

In this lush world where whispers abound,
I try to fit in, but feel like a clown.
Leaves and laughter make quite the affair,
Yet here I am, with stories to share!

Gardeners of the Soul

In pots of clay, we plant our dreams,
A little water, or so it seems.
With sunlight smiles, they stretch and grow,
But wait, is that a weed? Oh no!

We sing to them with pots in hand,
They wriggle roots, it's quite a band.
Yet sometimes they look back and glare,
Like, 'Dude, you forgot to share!'

We sprinkle love and whisper care,
In hopes that life's a love affair.
But every so often, green turns brown,
As if they're all wearing a frown!

So here's to plants, our leafy crew,
Who dance with us when skies are blue.
We may not always get it right,
But hey, they're still our great delight!

Wildflowers in the Living Room

In the corner stands a wild bouquet,
Thriving boldly, come what may.
A sunny patch with lots of flair,
While I knock over the chair!

They sway and dance, no cares at all,
While I bumble, trip and fall.
"Water me more!" they seem to cheer,
But how'd I spill it, oh dear, oh dear!

With every petal, a story blooms,
In quirky pots or silly rooms.
They roll their eyes at my green thumb,
As I remind them, "Relax, it's fun!"

So raise a glass to the flowers bold,
That laugh at troubles, never cold.
In this comical, cheerful spree,
They're wild enough for you and me!

Unfurling Dreams

In morning light, they stretch and yawn,
Each leaf a promise, beautifully drawn.
They peek at me, "What's next today?"
As I trip over the pot, oh yay!

Each curl and twist, a daring chance,
While I attempt a graceful dance.
A cactus sighs, "Just leave it be,"
"I'm spiky, dear, so don't hug me!"

The ferns all giggle, waving hello,
"Be careful there, we're not your show!"
With every sprawl, a laugh they sow,
A pantomime of joy and woe.

So let the plants unfurl with glee,
As we embrace this silly spree.
In mischievous blooms, they'll lead the way,
Together we'll brighten even the gray!

The Dance of Dust

Dust bunnies twirl on the window ledge,
While my plants gossip, I must allege.
"Who watered last?" the spider says,
"You know it's not me; I'm too busy!"

The dust, a party, on a gleaming leaf,
"Join us for fun, forget your grief!"
But I grab a cloth and swoosh it wide,
"Not today, dust, let's try to hide!"

The ferns roll their eyes and say with flair,
"Dust or no dust, we just don't care!"
With every sweep, they waltz away,
"Just try to clean up, if you may!"

So here's to dust, in its glorious form,
It adds a twist to the mundane norm.
In life's wild dance, we laugh and sway,
With plants and dust, it's a comical display!

Shadows of the Evergreen

In corners they plot, the leafy bunch,
Whispering secrets over the lunch.
"Do I need water?" one asks with glee,
While another sighs, "Not me, not me!"

They shuffle their pots with a wobble and sway,
Pretending to bask in the sun's golden ray.
Cactus rolls eyes, declares, "Not my style!"
While fern tries to dance, although just for a while.

A Pot for Every Memory

This old terracotta, a relic so grand,
Holds stories of leaves that danced hand in hand.
"Remember the puppy?" one succulent cried,
"You chewed on my petals, you thought it was fried!"

A pot for the cactus with prickles and pride,
"Less hugs!" it demands, "I'm not a joyride!"
"Combine me with soil, and let's build a dream,
Of tiny green kingdoms where we can all beam!"

The Revival of Roots

Who knew plants could party? They're wild and free,
Roots in a tangle, sipping on tea.
"I swear I'm a flower!" the weed shouts in jest,
While the orchid rolls eyes, "Just let's be our best!"

Moss on the shelf claims it's the new queen,
"Don't step on my throne, it's not fit for the green!"
Every leaf's a diva, with thoughts of their own,
As vines weave a tale that has truly grown.

The Texture of Time

Each leaf tells a story, some crinkled, some soft,
With gossip of growth, both upward and oft.
"I was here first," boasts a plant with a frown,
While the new sprout just giggles, "Look at me now!"

Dust bunnies gather, a sight to behold,
In the shadows of green, their tales are retold.
"Did you hear about Charlie, the plant that can't die?
We call him 'Immortal' – he's got quite the sly.

Green Chronicles

In a pot on the sill, looking so grand,
A succulent dreams of a rock band.
Water me? Nah, just a few drops.
I'm thriving here, it's just lip pops.

Cacti complain, 'What's with the fuss?'
While orchids roll eyes, 'Don't bother us!'
When the cat tries to nibble my leaves,
I shake my head, 'What a tease!'

Spider plants dance like they're in a show,
"More light, more love!" they holler and glow!
But when the sun hides, oh what a sight,
They sulk and act like it's the end of the night.

In this jungle of pots, we play our game,
Just try to keep me, you'll never be the same.
So here's to us, the green folks at play,
Living life leafy, come join the fray!

Leaves of Solitude

In corners I lurk, with a leaf like a fan,
Watching humans with their daily plan.
They talk to me like I've got a clue,
I just nod and soak up the dew.

A fern in the bathroom, it's quite the scene,
While the shower sings songs, I'm feeling all green.
'Hey, where's my root beer?' a rogue leaf will tease,
We laugh and we giggle, oh do what you please!

A lonely peace lily attracts all the flies,
'I'm just here for the drips!' it slyly replies.
When a mosquito checks in, all warily cool,
The lily just smiles, 'You're playing the fool!'

Here in my corner, I'll watch and I'll sigh,
Planet Earth's wild, I'm just living to try.
With pots full of stories, I'm never alone,
In this room of adventure, I've made a home!

Whispering Ferns

Whispering secrets with delicate fronds,
Ferns take their time, play their own songs.
Handle with care, they sway like a wisp,
Gossiping softly, their leaves twist and twist.

One cheeky leaf says, 'Why stay in your pot?
I dream of wild jungles, give it a shot!'
'The sun's too bright for us,' an elder leaf sighs,
'We prefer indirect, that's just how we rise.'

In the shade of the window, we dance with the breeze,
With emerald laughter that never does cease.
'Who needs a partner?' I proudly proclaim,
'We have each other, and ferns feel the same!'

So if you stop by, remember this dance,
You'll find us giggling, we like to take a chance.
In our leafy enclave, with stories to share,
We're the whispering ferns, in our own little air!

Sunlight's Embrace

Sunshine streams down, oh what a delight,
Dancing and swaying, we bask in the light.
A little too much? I feel rather burnt,
But give me that glow, and I'll never be spurned.

Windowsill crew, we're kings and queens,
Living for rays, flaunting our greens.
But then comes the shade, my frown goes deep,
'Without sunlight, what's a plant need to keep?'

We roast in the warmth but cringe in the cool,
Spinach has told me, 'Don't be such a fool!'
Yet here I stand, with a sunbeam parade,
We've all got our quirks; it's why we've stayed made.

So here's to the beams that warm our small hearts,
In this light-filled world where laughter imparts.
Join in the fun, plant pals in the race,
With sunlight's embrace, we make our own space!

Vignettes of Verdancy

In the corner sits a cactus, bold,
With needles prickly, stories untold.
A fern beside it shakes its fronds,
While mocking the sun for all that it bonds.

A tiny plant in a teacup's grace,
Sips on sunlight, finds its place.
While succulents roll their eyes in glee,
Plotting escape—oh, can't you see?

The spider plant, a webby sage,
Complains of rentals at this age.
"I need a window, fresh and bright,
Not this dim cupboard, not tonight!"

Each leaf a tale, each pot a laugh,
Water them well! They'll tell you half.
Green gossip flows, a leafy spree,
In our happy home, wild and free.

Solace in the Soil

Dirt under nails, a gardener's thrill,
Potted dreams and the chill of the drill.
A seedling whispers, 'Give me a chance!'
While weeds plot a rebellious dance.

"Watch out for me, I'm a sneaky sprout!"
Said the robust chives with a cheeky shout.
As daisies giggle in glittery pride,
"I'm the flower queen! You can't hide!'

Nestled in earth, with worms as friends,
Each bloom's a tale that never ends.
Join in the mess, embrace the grime,
For plant life's chaos is simply sublime!

With spades and laughter, we can't go wrong,
Planting our whims, we'll dance along.
So grab a pot and a friendly gnome,
In this glorious garden, we call home!

Whispers from the Fern

Opaque whispers sung by the fern,
"Please don't water! Just wait your turn."
Each frond a flag, so delicate,
Yet giggles echo, feeling quite great!

If humidity's right, oh what a treat,
The leaves all shimmer, they come alive, neat!
'Midst the wise succulents, they plot their schemes,
Dreaming of sunlight and curating dreams.

The pothos dances, climbs up the wall,
Says, "More light, please, I'm ready to sprawl!"
While smiling orchids eye the shelf,
Swaying with pride, each in its own self.

Together they giggle, a leafy parade,
In this wild home where laughter's made.
So raise a toast with your watering can,
To the secrets and joys of this plant-filled clan!

Sunlit Sanctuary Secrets

In the window's warm embrace,
A succulent's grin, such a bright face.
'I've got a secret, come close to hear,'
Said the reluctant snake plant with a sly sneer.

"Every leaf tells a story, you see,
Of nights spent dreaming, just like me!"
A cheerful philodendron adds with flair,
"With a touch of sunlight, I'm beyond compare!"

"Remember the time you forgot to feed?
I nearly wilted, planted deep in need!"
Chortled the jade with a mischievous wink,
"We share these tales over drinks—don't you think?"

As shadows stretch with the setting sun,
These earthly jesters have plenty of fun.
So tiptoe softly, listen and sway,
To the sunlit secrets of another day!

Echoes of Eden

In a pot so small, with roots that twist,
A fern that thinks it's hard to miss.
It dances in the morning light,
Thinking it's the garden's knight.

A cactus pricks with prickly glee,
'No water for me, can't you see?'
While succulents laugh in their green clothes,
Sharing secrets that no one knows.

A mischievous vine climbs up the wall,
Hoping one day it'll grow so tall.
Yet tripping over a shoelace strand,
It flops right down— oh, what a band!

Each leaf a joke, each stem a pun,
Growing together, just for fun.
In the house where silliness blooms,
Echoes of Eden fill all the rooms.

Secrets of the Seedling

In the corner, a seedling peeks,
With hopes and dreams, it gently shrieks.
'One day I'll reach the sun so bright!'
While soil whispers, 'Take it light!'

A sproutish thing with leaves a-twitch,
Contemplates the life of a rich witch.
Wishing for a potion or two,
To sprout up high, oh how it grew!

The sun laughs down, 'You're not quite ripe!'
While others whisper, 'Gotta hype!'
They plot and plan their leafy schemes,
Filling the air with self-made dreams.

But all the roots just roll their eyes,
Exchanging truth— no need for lies.
In this garden of thoughts freely spun,
The secrets grow wild, but all in fun.

The Narratives of Nature

In a teacup, a tiny tale unfolds,
Of plants that dream of hitting gold.
A mint that thinks it's all the rage,
While basil plays the wise old sage.

"Oh dear leaves, just hang on tight,"
Says the violet in a floral fight.
A battle over window light,
With comical twists as day turns night.

The ferns all giggle, clutching their fronds,
While chatting 'bout their leafy bonds.
"Who knew that chlorophyll could shine,
In such a wacky, leafy line?"

So when you visit, don't be shy,
Join the giggles as the leaves sway high.
These narratives of nature spin,
A comedy show— let's begin!

Whispers from the Windowsill

On the sill, the potted pals convene,
With stories tall and leaves so green.
A rubber plant claims it's quite a star,
While others note the restaurant jar.

A spider plant's in a twist of fate,
Swooning over how to propagate.
"I'm the one with the real debut!"
But all agree, they all look good too.

As sunlight drifts, they share their dreams,
Of garden gnomes and leafy themes.
"Who needs a gardener to approve?"
When nature's humor makes them move.

So lean in close and join their fun,
Whispers blend— now the day is done.
Among the pots, true laughter springs,
In windowsill chats, where joy takes wings.

The Hummingbird's Haven

In the corner, a pot of green,
Tiny blooms, a vivid scene.
Hummingbirds dance, a feathery plight,
I swear they're having a garden night!

Leaves rustle, a joke to share,
Is that a bug? No, just fresh air!
Water drips, it's like a flood,
Who knew I'd be a plant mom stud?

Fertilizer spills, a tragic fall,
My shoes are wrecked but my plants stand tall.
Gossip flows from leaf to leaf,
"Who's that? A friend or just a thief?"

Sunshine filters, bright and bold,
The plants and I, we share the gold.
With laughter, we bend, we grow,
In our haven, oh what a show!

Through the Windowpane

Peeking through my window's glass,
A jungle blooms—a cheeky sass!
Cacti pose like they own the place,
While leafy folks hold a poker face.

The fern waves as if to flirt,
"Come on out, you lush-rooted dirt!"
But out I stay, my snacks in hand,
Remarkable—how plants understand!

Outside, rain begins to pitter,
Inside, I watch, a cozy sitter.
"Look at us thrive!" they seem to shout,
Inside, outside—what's this about?

One day, I swear we'll trade a glance,
Go on a field trip—take a chance.
But for now, it's me and my view,
Each plant a secret, a leafy crew!

Sowing Serenity

In pots of dreams, I toss some seeds,
Water them well—ignore the weeds.
Each sprout's a giggle, a little tease,
"Bet you can't catch me!" they say with ease.

Garden gnomes chuckle, it's plain to see,
They're shocked, entranced by my history.
I trip on a spade, fall to my knees,
Plants laugh uproarious—oh, what a tease!

Sunshine dapples, lighting the lane,
A snail's slow dance keeps me entertained.
With every plant, there's a mishap told,
Yet in their presence, I feel bold.

Nature's riddle, this home of green,
Amidst chaotic joy, my heart's serene.
In mess and mirth, we tend our plot,
With every bloom, we laugh a lot!

The Art of Pruning

Snip, snip here, a little trim,
Oh no, there goes a branch so slim!
"Don't cry yet!" chirps my cactus friend,
"Just means more growth, so do not bend!"

Scissors gleam, it's quite a sight,
Chopping chaos feels so right.
"Let's shape up!" I hear the leaves sing,
"Who needs a stylist? We're the real bling!"

Ozzy the orchid hides in dismay,
"Will you do this with care today?"
With laughter, I say, "You'll look divine,"
As I duck from the ribbon-tied vine.

With every chop, a giggle erupts,
Is it nap time or art? Who disrupts!
Through prunings, friendships blossom anew,
This leafy life splits into a lively hue!

The Quiet Elegance of Ivy

In a corner it sprawls, a leafy delight,
Climbing the walls without fuss or fright.
Whispers of green in the sun's gentle hug,
Who knew a plant could give such a shrug?

Spilling down vessels, a graceful cascade,
Ivy's just here for the free sunlight trade.
Tales of romance with each tendril it weaves,
Who needs a partner when you've got good leaves?

Trailing and wrapping, it circles with glee,
As if it knows all the secrets of me.
A little salute, in the morning's soft glow,
My leafy confidant, quiet and slow.

In a pot there's a world, so busy and grim,
While I sip my coffee, it just leans in,
A life of leisure and knowing just when,
To bask in the sun, or go back again.

Echoes of Eden in a Tiny Room

A fern on the shelf, with a style that's divine,
Waves at the dust bunnies, feeling quite fine.
With each tiny frond, it demands a salute,
"Hey, wake up, humans! Put down the old loot!"

Cacti in rows, like a prickly parade,
Each one a soldier, their patience displayed.
When I water too much, they stand there with glares,
As if they're saying, "Find someone who cares!"

The snake plant's sulking, its leaves in a pout,
"Why does that snail get all the best clout?"
While over in the corner the orchids just tease,
"Bloom where you're planted," they say with a breeze.

In the midst of the clutter, their joy is a must,
Each leaf is a story of grit and of trust.
In this enchanted realm, what a funny show,
Eden's whispers fill the space, don't let them go!

Sprouts of Wisdom

A sprout in a pot, with wisdom to share,
"Water me gently, if you really care."
Its tiny green leaves, a sage in disguise,
Whispers of patience in each morning's rise.

A succulent cheerleader, bold and so bright,
Shouts, "Chill out, dude, bask in the light!"
While the basil nearby is plotting a plan,
Demanding respect like a true herbivore fan.

The beetroot just giggles, a round little jester,
"Root deep in the soil! I'm a true investor!"
But alas, in the end, they all seem to tease,
The dark side of sunlight—too much, and you freeze!

So here in my garden, they teach me all day,
Life's a comedy show, what more can I say?
Learn from the greens, as they dance and they sway,
Even a cabbage finds humor at play.

Reflections in a Glass Terrarium

Inside a glass dome, there's a party in style,
Moss squishes in corners, all green and a smile.
Succulents peep out, with a glimmer of sass,
"Check out this view, dude! It's truly first-class!"

The tiny stones whisper of journeys they've made,
"Once I was on a river, now I just fade."
While the ferns in the back toss their fronds in the air,
"More light over here! We're the ultimate flare!"

Humidity levels are soaring with glee,
As earthworms retell their wild, wiggly spree.
Ladybugs giggle and chase little flies,
In here, anyone can be wise in disguise.

So closely they cling, these friends made of green,
Sharing their secrets, as if it's routine.
With laughter in soil, and joy in each leaf,
My glassy oasis, a true weird relief!

Petals in the Windowlight

In the sun, they dance and sway,
Catching rays in a playful way.
Spilling soil like it's confetti,
Oh dear, my plant is looking petty!

Whispers of water, they call my name,
Daily tussles, it's all a game.
Each leaf's a selfie, all green and proud,
While I'm just lost in a leafy crowd.

A spider plant steals my precious space,
It thinks it's winning this leafy race.
Poking out leaves like it's been in gym,
I swear its ego is getting grim!

Yet with each sprout, I laugh and groan,
My plant collection has overgrown.
A jungle of joy, a funny mess,
At least I'm never in distress!

The Language of Leaves

Oh, the gossip those leaves must share,
In quiet tones, floating in the air.
A succulent says, "I'm low maintenance!"
While ferns whisper, "It's all about patience!"

An orchid's drama in full bloom,
With petals glistening like an heirloom.
"Just look at me! I'm quite the sight!"
While cacti smirk, "I can hold a fight!"

Bantering roots beneath the ground,
In their secret world, surprises abound.
But when I trip on a wayward vine,
They chuckle softly, their roots entwined!

So next time you see a plant or two,
Remember, they're scheming just like you.
With every leaf in green attire,
They'll spread their tales, like wires on fire!

Roots Beneath the Surface

Underneath in the dark they creep,
Rooted secrets, quiet and deep.
"Are you feeding us?" they always plea,
While I just wonder what's next on TV!

Tangled stories in earthen beds,
Whispers of dreams dancing in reds.
A blame game starts when pots overfill,
Now there's mud, and my fingers chill.

"Oh, why are you so clingy today?"
But those roots just giggle, "We love the sway!"
Every new shoot sprouts with glee,
While I'm left wrestling with my own spree.

So pot me a mix of humor and cheer,
With roots that waltz, my plants sincere.
I'll nurture them well, but let's not forget,
They'll trick me again, of that, I bet!

A Symphony of Chlorophyll

In harmony, the greens unfold,
A concert hall of stories told.
Each leaf a note in nature's song,
While I join in, but often wrong!

A fern that fronds like it's doing a dance,
While the pothos hops, given the chance.
A nightly opera of water and light,
Too loud for neighbors, it's quite the sight!

The jade plant hums a robust tune,
While succulents chime under the moon.
But when I trip on a rogue leaf stray,
They all erupt in gleeful dismay!

So here's to the fun, the laughs we share,
In this leafy world, beyond compare.
With sunlight as our ultimate friend,
We'll symphonize until the very end!

Chronicles of the Potted Realm

In the corner sits a fern,
Plotting plots of green concern.
A cactus winks, I swear it's true,
Planning pricks for all who strew.

A spider plant claims the shelf,
Says, "You'll water me yourself!"
With every droop and curl it says,
"I thrive on negligence for days!"

The violets gossip quite a lot,
Discussing which one's got the spot.
"Look at me, I'm blooming bright!"
But it's the weeds that steal the light!

In this realm of pots and smiles,
We dance with bugs in leafy files.
With every frond and every leaf,
We laugh at life, prepare for grief.

Leaves and Lullabies

In a sunny nook, the pothos sings,
Swaying gently, like it has wings.
A tune it croons, with photosynthesis,
"Feed me sun, and I'll grant you bliss!"

The rubber plant just rolls its eyes,
Wishing for some cooler skies.
"It's too hot, I'm melting here!"
While the air ferns whip, "No fear!"

Spare me the fuss, says the lucky bamboo,
"I'm in feng shui, don't you know?"
All the others just laugh and scoff,
"You'll be the first that we'll toss!"

With every drop of morning dew,
We sing for joy, the whole day through.
In our garden of silly dreams,
We craft our tales, we weave our schemes.

Succulent Dreams and Soil Tales

A succulent dreams of a sunny shore,
"I crave some warmth, give me more!"
With little spines and hopes held tight,
It plans a trip, but won't take flight.

The soil grumbles, "I'm getting tired!"
"Why can't you two be more inspired?"
It wants some jazz, some daily songs,
Instead, it sits while the plant prolongs.

A jade plant bakes under a lamp,
"I'm such a prize, but oh so cramp!"
It dreams of space, a vast and grand,
But here it sits, with roots all planned.

We giggle at our little plight,
Every wilt and fall feels just right.
In our potting party, nothing's wrong,
We laugh and sway to the plant song!

Green Guardians of Indoor Realms

Beneath the light, a hero stands,
An aloe vera with healing hands.
"I've got your back for every burn,
But sugar water? You never learn!"

The snake plant sways with regal flair,
"I'm low maintenance, if you dare!"
While the rubber plant scoffs in disdain,
"Just give me love, or feel the pain!"

Potted sentinels of sorts,
We guard our space with leafy forts.
Every glance, a swagger, a grin,
"We grow together, let's begin!"

With jokes and jives, we share our fate,
In this plant world, we celebrate.
In pots so small, our spirits soar,
Join us here, you'll ask for more!

Tales from the Terracotta

In a pot with soil so rich,
Sits a plant, a quirky niche.
Whispers secrets, grows so bold,
Turns to gold in morning's hold.

Water spills, a sloshy tide,
A leaf peeks out, insists on pride.
"Not too much!" I try to say,
Yet he flourishes anyway!

Mischievous roots begin to creep,
Making my flowerbed a heap.
I chuckle, what a daring feat,
The pot's a throne, oh how sweet!

Every morning, what a sight,
Leaves all laughing in the light.
They might mock my brownish thumb,
But hey, they dance when I hum!

Resilient Green Companions

In my room, the plants conspire,
Growing taller, they never tire.
One threw a party, what a scene,
With tiny lights, all decked in green.

I bought one fancy, full of flair,
It wilted fast, it didn't care.
"Just a phase!" I told my friend,
Next week it burst, what a trend!

A cactus grinned, so full of pride,
With spikes that kept all pests outside.
"Come closer!" it dared with glee,
As I tiptoed past, grinning with glee.

Together we laugh, dark or bright,
In each window basking in light.
These leafy pals, such joyful luck,
Who needs a dog? I'm all plant-struck!

The Dance of the Jade Plant

A jade plant sways, what a move,
With leaves that gleam, oh how they groove.
I catch it dancing on the shelf,
I swear it jives just like myself!

Singing softly, a little tune,
Under the glow of the big full moon.
Each leaf a partner, twirling around,
Making mischief without a sound.

"Do you need water?" I tease and jest,
"Only if you promise to give it your best!"
With every sip, it gives a nod,
Seems impressed with every prod.

Oh, the jade knows, it's true indeed,
How joy can sprout from simple heed.
With laughter shared, we revel and play,
A wacky duo at end of the day!

Nature's Quiet Observers

In the corner, plants sit and stare,
Watching me lounge, without a care.
Their leaves waggle, a subtle cheer,
Can they see my snacks, so near?

Just the other day I slipped,
Tripped over a pot, man, I flipped!
They shook with giggles, oh what fun,
Nature's laughter, I heard them run.

Each morning, they whisper, "Rise!"
Encouraging me with tiny sighs.
While I sip tea, they blink and plot,
Dreaming adventures on the spot.

These silent friends, with much to say,
I often wonder what they portray.
In their green worlds, I can't outsmart,
Nature's quiet, hilarious art!

Heartbeats in Clay

In the corner, a succulent sighs,
With a smile just slightly askew.
Lettuce pondered why it wore a hat,
Cactus chuckled, 'It's a fashion debut!'

A fern that thinks it's a diva star,
Perched atop an ancient pot.
'Look at me, I'm so lush and green!'
While spider plant shrieks, 'Not really, it's not!'

Potted pals with quirky pose,
Dance and sway in the sunlight glow.
Each leaves a trail of dirt behind,
'It's a mud mask, now let it flow!'

As night falls upon our leafy crew,
They gossip about the day's delight.
'He spilled his drink, isn't he a klutz!'
And that's how they party all night!

Roots Beneath the Surface

In the soil where secrets dwell,
Roots giggle and wiggle away.
'More water please,' the brambles tease,
'If I grow taller, I'll steal the day!'

Worms whisper tales of their soil lives,
'You think your leaves are all that grand?'
But the roots beneath, they all connect,
In a club where no one makes demands.

Beneath the dirt, they play charades,
Pretending to be just another weed.
'Look at Dave, he's stretching wide!'
But he's really just fulfilling a need.

So if you find a flower sprout,
Remember what's hidden far below.
The laugh's not just in pretty blooms,
But in roots that put on quite the show!

The Tending Touch

Watering can heavy like a weight,
With a flick of the wrist, off we go.
'Just a drizzle, not a flood!'
But I get distracted by a garden gnome's glow.

With clippers in hand, a snip-snip here,
'Oh dear, should I trim or should I cheer?'
Chia pets squawk, 'Leave some for us!'
But it's those wild daisies I hold so dear.

Fertilizer sprinkled with glee,
'What's that smell? Did I drop a shoe?'
The houseplants laugh, 'It's just a treat!'
And I'm the one who's feeling blue.

At the end of the day, all is well,
Though chaos reigned in my leafy plot.
With laughter in the leaves, so sweet,
It's a job where I connect a lot!

Flora's Journey

From shy sprouts to a brilliant tree,
Every day is an adventure born.
Napping potted palms whisper dreams,
Healing hands make all 'em feel reborn.

Cacti set sail on seas of light,
With a wild sense of humor in bloom.
'Watch me float!' they sing out loud,
'Let's make this pot our new cozy room!'

And every morning, they gather round,
Stretch and shake off the sleepy night.
It's a circus of color and charm,
Comedy in every sunbeam's light.

So here's to the winks and the twirls,
In pots where laughter grows like weeds.
The journey of plants is full of joy,
In their leafy lives, my heart proceeds!

Echoes of Nature's Heart

In the corner sits a fern,
Whispering secrets of green,
Every leaf a little tale,
Of wild dreams yet unseen.

The cactus cracks a joke,
While spitting thorns with glee,
"I may be prickly, friend,
But I'm a riot, don't you see?"

Pothos climbs and takes a leap,
Swaying like it's in a dance,
"I'll take the high road, thank you,
And give this place a chance!"

Oh, the laughter in the leaves,
With each new day that dawns,
A jungle full of humor,
In quiet, leafy lawns.

Symphony of Succulents

In shadows lurk small wonders,
Tiny pots stacked high,
They snicker in the sunlight,
As if they own the sky.

The jade plant jests with riches,
"Look at my shiny loot!"
While aloe holds a concert,
"I'll soothe you with a root!"

Echeveria wears a crown,
Swaying with such flair,
"I'm the queen of water storage,
Does anyone even care?"

Together they create a tune,
A melody of green,
In the quirky world of foliage,
Where laughter reigns supreme.

The Color of Renewal

Oh, the joy of sprouting leaves,
Bright greens from winter's gloom,
Bouncing back with vibrant hues,
In the cozy living room.

A single bloom defies the odds,
Pushing forth from a brown pot,
"Look at me! I'm a flower!"
"I sure had a funny thought!"

The soil scoffs and cheers them on,
"We're all a little twisted here!"
While roots dance in the dark,
"Cheers to growth, my dears!"

With every petal's opening,
A laugh escapes the air,
Nature's jesters at their best,
In potting soil, we share.

Hidden Harvest

A string of pearls hangs low,
With a glinting, playful sheen,
"I'm like a rolling treasure hunt,
In the jungle of your green!"

The basil plots a scheme,
"Let's spice up this old meal!"
With every leaf, a giggle,
"You can't resist my zeal!"

The thyme winks with wisdom,
"Slow down, dear friend, and see,"
"Every moment's ripe and ready,
For medicinal glee!"

In pots of quirky wonders,
A harvest full of fun,
So laugh with quirky foliage,
Underneath the shining sun.

Secrets of the Soil

Beneath the pot, a secret lies,
Worms hold meetings, planning spies.
They gossip of who needs a drink,
And how to make the roots all shrink.

Fungus adds flavor, just for flair,
While beetles dance without a care.
The soil's a club where all belong,
With no need for a fancy song.

The gardener thinks it's all serene,
But underground, it's quite the scene.
They plot their pranks on every sprout,
And laugh when plants scream, "Get me out!"

Next time you water, take a peek,
There's mischief brewing, so to speak.
Remember, dirt's not just for show,
It's where the fun and secrets flow.

The Flight of a Spider Plant

A spider plant dreams of the sky,
"I'll sprout some wings and learn to fly!"
With leaves like wings, it takes its shot,
While hanging high, it ties a knot.

It swings and sways in the warm breeze,
Like a hang glider with such ease.
But oh dear, what a funny sight,
It tangled with a bird in flight!

Down it dangles, all in a twist,
Crying, "Someone save me, I insist!"
The bird just chirps, "This is your fate,
You can't soar high, just cultivate!"

So, it learns to relax in its pot,
Finding joy in the mess it's got.
No need for wings to feel delight,
Just stretching out in the soft sunlight.

Guardians of the Green

In the corner stands a fierce fern,
With leaves that threaten, "You'll get burned!"
A rubber plant plays the wise old sage,
While cacti laugh, saying, "Turn the page!"

Succulents gather round for tea,
"Let's plot our escape from this glee!"
They whisper softly, share their schemes,
To invade the kitchen filled with dreams.

The snake plant grumbles, "I'm still here,
Keeping watch with my stalks so clear."
"Yet if they water, we could all drown,
Let's stick together, don't wear a frown!"

Together they stand, a leafy crew,
Defending their territory, that's what they do.
So bow to the guardians of green mayhem,
For laughter and life, they're the ultimate gem!

Resilience in Pottery

A pot cracked wide, but holds its ground,
With dirt inside, it won't back down.
Plants poke out, in comical poses,
Saying, "We make the best of roses!"

"Look at me," said the chubby jade,
"Though cracked, I thrive; my colors invade!
Resilience is our finest trait,
We laugh at fate and dance with fate."

A broken pot, a tale to spin,
Each chip and flaw is where we win.
"This rustic charm," the ferns declare,
"Means we've got stories and we don't care!"

So raise your pots, be proud, rejoice,
In the cracks, you'll hear us voice,
The humor life spills in dirt and clay,
We'll bloom regardless, come what may!

In Praise of Petunias

Petunias dance in the wind's embrace,
With colors bright, they twirl and chase.
Their petals giggle, a floral joke,
Dressed to the nines, both glam and bespoke.

Oh, how they whisper sweet nothings at night,
Enticing bugs with their floral delight.
"Come sip our nectar!" they sing in a tune,
While I just roll my eyes, they're quite the cartoon.

Each morning I see them, with faces so bold,
Reminding me daily that life's to be sold.
"Buy your own sunshine!" their mantra declared,
Yet all I wanted was a flower to be shared.

So here's to petunias, with cheeky grins,
In pots of laughter, where fun never thins.
With friendships like these, who needs a grand plan?
Just a splash of color—let the joy span!

Chronicles of Chlorophyll

Once in a pot where the sunlight would gleam,
Lived a leafy rogue with a wild green dream.
"I'm epic!" it boasted, "In photosynthesis art,
My blades are my canvas, behold my fine heart!"

But every time I forgot to hydrate,
It would droop and sulk, oh the tantrum it'd create!
All puffed up like royalty, it taught me the way,
To treat my greens right or face disarray.

Friends turned to ferns, we often convened,
Composing our tales of the sunlight we gleaned.
With snickers and whispers, we'd weave quite a plot,
How roots rule the world and why soil's so hot.

But one blustery day, a leaf blew away,
And the plant screamed loudly, "That's just not okay!"
Yet with a bit of water and some love from my hand,
Chlorophyll's chronicles would continue to stand.

The Urban Oasis

In the city's heart, we sprout and rejoice,
A funky green squad, quite a chirpy voice.
With pots piled high on each windowsill ledge,
We dream of a world that's free from the dredge.

Cacti raise arms, wearing spikes as a crown,
While ferns roll their eyes at our urban showdown.
Together we laugh, a household of cheer,
"Water me, love me!" we chant to appear.

A rogue spider plant hangs down with ambition,
"Just call me the king of this leafy condition!"
While succulents smirk, all chubby and wise,
"Chill out," they say, "We're the cool kids, no lies!"

But when guests arrive to admire our flair,
We bristle with pride, leaving them gasping air.
"Oh, what an oasis!" they chuckle and jest,
Yet really, it's just us, in our green fashion fest!

Nature's Quiet Companions

On shelves they meander, with whispers so soft,
The houseplants stand guard, oh so gently aloft.
They nod to the rhythm of each passing day,
While I brew my coffee in the usual way.

Oh, how they listen, attentive and true,
To tales of my woes and my dreams, just a few.
With leaves full of wisdom, they nod their sweet heads,
"I'm here for you, buddy, now just mind your threads."

But when nighttime falls and the dim lights do glow,
They sneak in a chuckle and a quick leafy show.
"Remember that time you forgot us again?
We staged a revolt, your very own zen!"

So here's to the plants, they're my quirky best friends,
With humor and heart, on them I depend.
In a world full of chaos, they're all that I need,
Nature's quiet companions, planting joy like a seed!

www.ingramcontent.com/pod-product-compliance
Lightning Source LLC
Chambersburg PA
CBHW072133070526
44585CB00016B/1652